APPRECIATING ALL OF THE CONTINENTS

CHILDREN'S MODERN HISTORY

Speedy Publishing LLC
40 E. Main St. #1156
Newark, DE 19711
www.speedypublishing.com

Do you know about the continents, the great bodies of land separated by oceans on our planet Earth? Do you know their names, and which one your country belongs to? Well, let's find out!

The Earth, and all its wonders, is comprised of seven continents.
Wait... rewind.

What are continents, you might ask?

continents

NORTH AMERICA

EUROPE

AFRICA

SOUTH AMERICA

ASIA

AUSTRALIA

The word “continent” comes from the Latin word “continere”, meaning “to hold together”. It’s a large continuous mass of land.

Since our Earth has seven continents, we'll look at them one by one—from the largest to the smallest in size. The seven-continent model is commonly taught in schools and used in scientific contexts.

ASIA

Asia covers about 9% of the Earth's surface. It is subdivided into forty-eight countries, according to the United Nations. It is also the most populated continent. This continent also is extremely diverse, both in climates and geographic features.

AFRICA

The world's second largest with the oldest populated areas. There are fifty-four countries. The different states and groups here have very distinct languages and customs. Sadly, this is considered as the poorest and most underdeveloped of the continents where people live.

Broadway
North Am

NORTH AMERICA

It was named after the Italian explorer, Americo Vespucci. One notable fact is that this continent is considered as the only one which has every kind of climate.

North America has twenty-three countries. It is home to the largest lake in the world (Lake Superior).

SOUTH AMERICA

This is one of the most amazing continents as it has so much to offer!

It cradles the natural wonders of the world with unique cultures and interesting histories:

- Angel Falls in Venezuela. This is the highest uninterrupted waterfall in the world.

- The Amazon River. It has the largest water volume of any river in the world.
- The Amazon Forest, the largest natural rainforest in the world.
- Andes Mountainsare the longest mountain range in the world.

ANTARCTICA

It comes from the Greek word which means "opposite to the north." It is the coldest landmass on earth, with beautiful permanent glaciers.

ANTARCTICA

It is the least populated continent with very few plant and animal species. The only people on Antarctica are visiting scientists.

EUROPE

The earth's largest continent. This is where several great advances in human history originated that had a huge influence over the world, like the Renaissance and the Industrial Revolution.

ope
gian Sea
North Sea
Norway
Sweden
Finland
Russia
Estonia
Latvia
Lithuania
Belarus
Denmark
United Kingdom
Netherlands
Belgium
Germany
Poland
Czech Rep.
Slovakia
Austria
Hungary
Ukraine
Moldova
Romania
Switzerland
France
Italy
Croatia
Bosnia and Herzegovina
Serbia
Bulgaria
Macedonia
Albania
Greece
Black Sea
Turkey
Spain

FRANCE
IRELAND
GERMANY
SPAIN
UK
GREECE
SWEDEN
ITALY

Some of the world's greatest empires were also founded here. There are more than 250 distinct languages spoken in Europe.

AUSTRALIA

The single country continent or island continent. It is popularly termed as the country "down under."

Australia

CONTINENTS OF THE WORLD

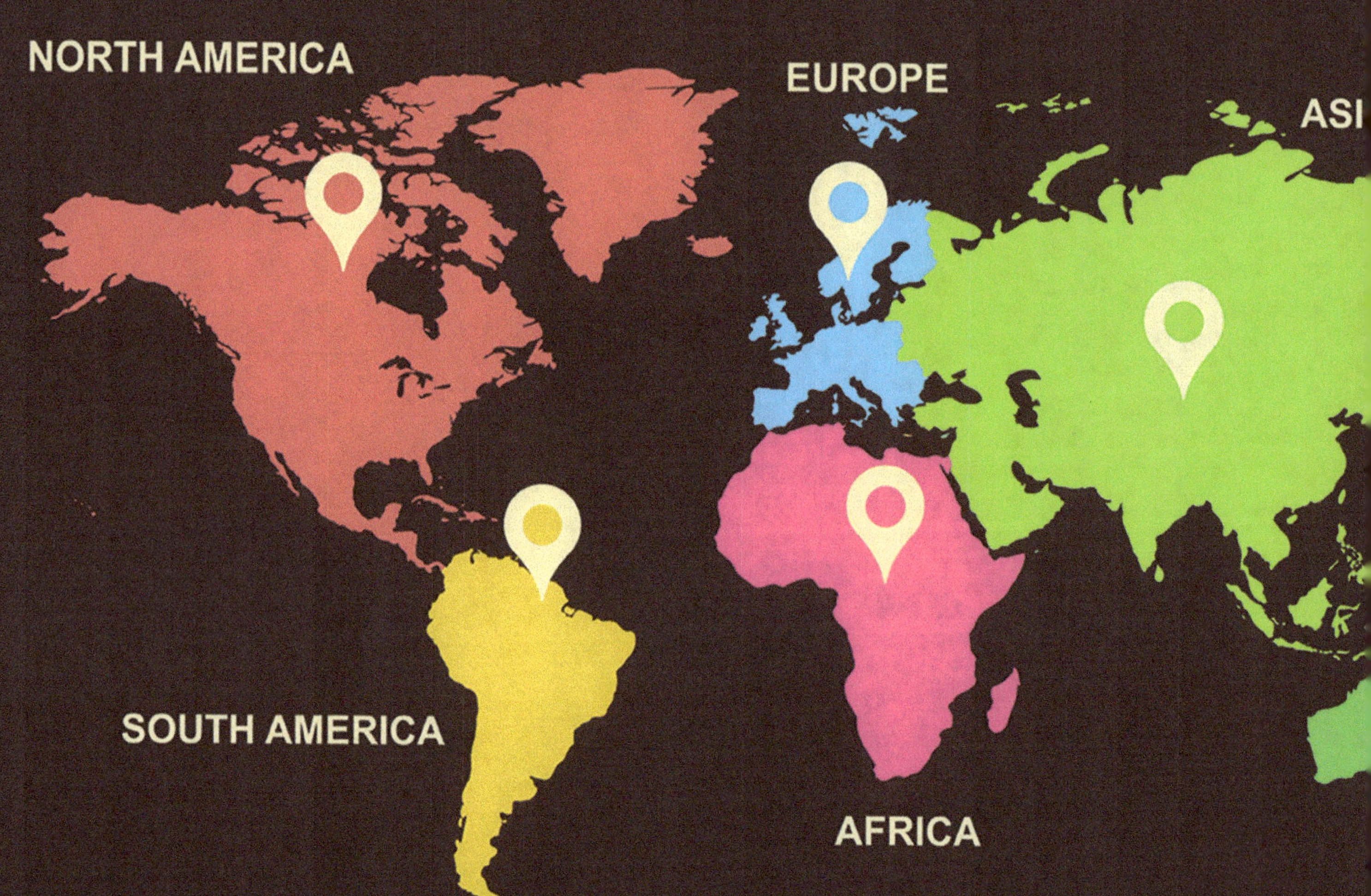

Australia is the smallest of all seven continents. But, as small as it may seem, it is where the Great Barrier Reef, the largest coral reef in the world, is located.

There you have it—all seven continents! As you now know the names and a few details of each of the continents, get a map or globe and see if you can find each one!

MAP OF THE WORLD
Arctic Ocean
Europe
Asia
Atlantic Ocean
Pacific Ocean
Africa
Indian Ocean
Australia
Antarctica

ARCTIC OCEA
NORTH AMERICA
EUROPE
ASIA
ATLANTIC OCEAN
PACIFIC OCEAN
AFRICA
SOUTH AMERICA
INDIAN OCEAN
ANTARCTICA

Can you find your own country? Which continent is it part of? Appreciate and have fun!

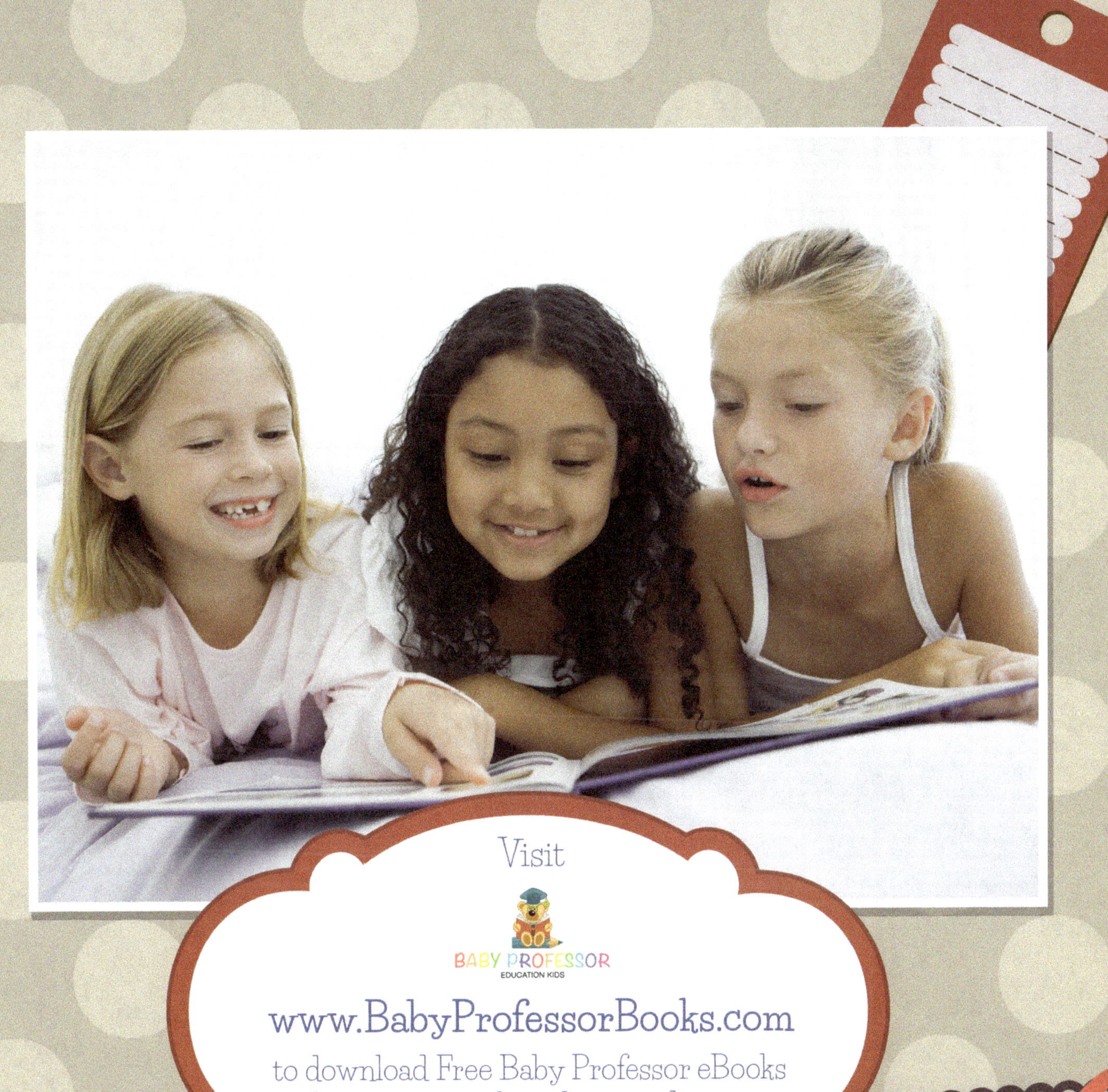

www.ingramcontent.com/pod-product-compliance
Lightning Source LLC
LaVergne TN
LVHW060830170826
845678LV00010B/1946

* 9 7 9 8 8 6 9 4 4 4 2 7 1 *